A Seamless LIFE

RESTING IN
God's Plan for You

A
Seamless
LIFE

RESTING IN
God's Plan for You

LYNDIE METZ

Published by Redemption Press, PO Box 427, Enumclaw, WA 98022
Toll Free (844) 2REDEEM (273-3336)

Redemption Press is honored to present this title in partnership with the author. The views expressed or implied in this work are those of the author. Redemption Press provides our imprint seal representing design excellence, creative content, and high quality production.

ISBN 13: 978-1-68314-798-5
ePub ISBN: 978-1-68314-799-2
Kindle ISBN: 978-1-68314-800-5
Library of Congress Catalog Card Number: 2019936639

TABLE OF CONTENTS

ACKNOWLEDGEMENTS

To ANDY, SANDRA, and the entire North Point Community Church Team,
Thank you for creating environments where this wandering sinner was not afraid to plug in and experience God for real for the first time ever. I truly have no idea where I would be without you.

To DAVE, KATE, and the entire Itown Church Team,
Thank you for following God's call to create a space to lead people from where they are to where God wants them to be. This wifey and mama of three needs community and support to draw closer to Him in everyday life. I look forward to continuing to serve with you all!

CHAPTER ONE

SEAMLESS BEGINNINGS

For I am about to do something new. See, I have already begun!

Do you not see it?

Isaiah 43:19

BEGINNINGS ARE AUTOMATIC—THEY just *happen*—and we don't realize their power until we ponder that beginning from somewhere in the middle or maybe even at the end. Once upon a time, I met my Prince Charming, fell in love, and got married. If, in the early days of wedded bliss, you'd have told me that my husband and I would not always see eye to eye on the most basic issues, I wouldn't have believed you. But those days of conflict did come. Somewhere in the middle of them, I realized how much the life we've always lived can affect the life we live today.

I began life in a loving home in a midsized Indiana town. My parents both worked outside the home, and my upbringing was comparable to that of other middle-class Midwestern girls. Not long after I arrived, my parents brought twins into the world: a boy and a girl. My traditional family has gone through ups and downs along the way, but the beginning was bliss.

Some of my earliest memories involve being in church. I remember singing "Down by the Creek Bank" and sitting up front with the pastor of our teeny tiny church before he dismissed us to junior church. I can still smell the real-butter grilled cheese sandwiches we ate at the church preschool as we got ready for our afternoon naps. I was under five, and these formative memories remain crystal clear. I'm sure the pastor and teachers planted seeds of God's love in me there, but religion and relationship seem to come at different times for different people. These things didn't click for me for a long time.

Although I attended church from a very young age, my family went through attendance spurts. Months often went by that I don't remember attending at all. I don't know why we were sporadic church attenders. Perhaps my parents didn't find a church connection or a place where they felt at home in God's house. Maybe they were just doing their best to raise babies in this crazy, busy world. Oh, if only someone would've shown them the power of a circle of believers around a young family!

After my preschool experiences, my next memories of church are from my late elementary years, when some neighborhood kids invited me to vacation Bible school. I went with them for at least a couple of summers, but I never attended their churches on Sundays or holidays because they didn't invite me to those services. I am the perfect example of evangelism consisting of nothing more than an invitation to church. Most likely, I would've gone, and I would have brought my whole family with me. I also have vague memories of a church camp I attended during one of those sit-this-one-out years for my family. This was my first camp experience, not to be revisited again until later in life when we were more grounded in our church and community. Again, God planted His seeds of love.

Finally, the Lord interacted with my family in an abrupt way. We had moved several times before I made it to the fifth grade. It seemed every time my dad got a promotion, we got a bigger and better house. Before the start of my sixth-grade year, we moved again, but this time something was different. We not only lived in a new house, but we started a new chapter as a family. Actually, quite a few chapters. We moved to another midsized town in central Indiana. This time, however, God placed us right next to a preacher. He and his family had just moved to town from California, and the ages of their children lined up perfectly with ours. This had to be a match made in heaven.

I'll never forget the first day my parents took us to visit our new house. When I saw the neighbors outside and discovered that the kids were friendly, I was excited to move. Every other time, I'd dreaded packing my belongings, attending a new school, and making new friends. But this time, God gave me built-in friends. I had hope. God used that first encounter to whisper, "You are safe here."

From the beginning of our relationship as neighbors, we kids got along well. Naturally, they invited us to church. And so we went—by ourselves at first. Our parents came later, but once we were all there, we stayed. God used that church and that family to speak into our lives and show us how to follow Him.

The guiding light of God's grace began as a genuine, nonjudgmental friendship. I believe that relationship nurtured change for us. The bond that developed put strong roots down into good soil. We became the closest friends with our neighbors—we studied the Bible, watched football, celebrated holidays, and ran around the neighborhood together. Our moms played cards at one house while our dads played video games at the other. We played all day until our parents called us in for dinner, and we met up again the next morning to do it all over again. I have the fondest memories of my childhood because God uprooted my family and placed us seamlessly where we belonged.

At the church we attended because our new friends issued their invitation, we learned about the love of Jesus and the importance of fellowship. My dad, my siblings, and I were baptized at that church. We all attended regularly and got involved in different areas of ministry throughout the church. We were infant Christians, and this time and place was our "introduction to solids."

If you are a parent, you know about that incredible yet treacherous time in an infant's life. Incredible because the baby branches out and experiences new flavors. Treacherous because the baby has to try some nasty stuff that's good for them. No matter the child's response, they can no longer survive on milk alone. They must eat something that will sustain them and help them grow. Some babies transition more easily than others. Even within my own little family, I have one child who wanted to eat everything and one who cared only for sweet potatoes.

Aren't we like that as Christians? Some are so on fire for Jesus right away that everyone immediately recognizes the change. Others just stick to their worship music in the car for months or years before anyone sees a difference.

My family had gotten by in life with a true belief in God and prayers before meals, but it was time for more. I wish I could say I "got it" right then and there. But the dots still hadn't connected yet for me. I went to church on Sundays, attended a Bible study at the neighbors' house on Wednesdays, and even went to church camp with the youth group every summer. When I understood the real meaning of Christ dying for my sins, I was baptized, but at that time, I didn't make a commitment to align my life with His.

I was a pretty good kid, afraid of getting into trouble. A natural-born rule follower, I can count on one hand the number of times I blatantly disobeyed my parents. I have a permanent reminder of one of those times: the ink under my skin. This choice severely upset and disappointed my mother. According to her, I had ruined my body, which is a temple of the Lord. Yes, and it still is, Mom.

You can go either way on your opinion of tattoos, and I don't mind which way you adopt.

I do know that I now have a time stamp of a life lived so selfishly that it never occurred to me to pray about my decisions. Sometimes we need reminders of our waywardness, so we can remember God loves us and is merciful despite our selfishness. We don't need reminders that keep us from God, but ones that make us thankful for His grace. In hindsight, I appreciate the metaphor of my selfishness that reminds me of my dependency on God, but did it have to be a cross between tribal and oceanic art? The joke's on me because I ended up with a tribute to Batman or Wu-Tang Clan—take your pick. God does have a sense of humor.

For me, *religion* began as early as I can remember. A *relationship with Christ*, on the other hand, didn't begin until I moved out and away from everything familiar. It's funny how the comforts of our own lives sometimes lead us to complacency. I was complacent.

Complacent people react in different ways. Some turn to light, and others turn to darkness. I knew God was calling me to more, yet I didn't know what or why or how I would get there. I wanted to be balanced, healthy, and whole. All the while, I lived day to day, unfulfilled, and empty. I can't trace my knowledge of that void back to a certain event or circumstance; it just hit me all at once.

I was in my second year of teaching elementary school. I was passionate about working with children and getting kids excited about learning, but I was ridiculously unhappy. Spiritually, I felt lost. I didn't even know where to begin. Physically, I was unhealthy. I paid no attention to my diet or exercise. I felt bad about myself but couldn't motivate myself to change. Emotionally, I was trying to do life on my own . . . and shutting out good people in the process.

I claimed great friendships but not with godly people. I pursued romantic relationships but not with God-fearing, churchgoing men. I thought I could live however I wanted and still get into heaven because I was saved. I didn't understand how we are to surrender our lives when we rest in salvation (John 15:13). God has much to do in and through us. If we simply pursue the world while claiming eternity in heaven, we will miss out miserably.

Mentally, I was drained. I was putting everything I had into my career every week and trying to drink away my cares on the weekends. I was fed up with myself.

Looking back, I see that those feelings of unrest were from the Holy Spirit, as He stirred me to something new. However, I didn't recognize that at the time. I had taken a personal hiatus from church attendance because I wanted to do life on my own without God's intervention. The only wisdom I was receiving was from my daily chats with my mom and the occasional sermonette from a sweet little lady at work.

Their words of truth encouraged me, but not so much that I wanted to make daily changes. I found comfort in my mom reminding me to "be still" during unsettling or uncertain times. I remember the spring in my coworker's step as she sang "Jesus Loves Me" in the hallways. I wasn't paying much attention, but God was working anyway. He uses everything for His glory. Everything. Even when we don't see the bigger picture, He is in control.

I was unhealthy and unhappy with my life, but I wasn't concerned enough to care. I sat on those feelings for about a year, pushing forward each day only because it was expected of me. And then came the unexpected death of one of my first-grade students. I'm sure what I went through was nothing compared with the loss his family must've felt, but I was devastated. God used this unfortunate experience to initiate my new beginning.

I remember finding out about his death. It doesn't matter if you are a student or a teacher—when you're summoned to the principal's office, the queasy feeling is the same. The secretary called my room to let me know I was needed in the office right away. She told me someone was coming to monitor my class while I met with the principal. Her voice sounded shaky, so I knew something was wrong. Frightfully wrong.

Little did I know how God was going to use the news I would receive. He was about to use the unfolding tragedy to seamlessly pull me out of my complacency and into a deep relationship with Him.

The next events are a bit of a blur. The call, the walk, the news—it all happened so fast. On my way to the office, I knew something wasn't right. I couldn't think of anything except those students I'd left in my classroom. Would they misbehave? Would they learn anything today? Would I have a bad report upon my return to the classroom?

But the bad report awaited me in the principal's office.

I went in and shut the door.

My student had been in a car accident. He'd been in the backseat with his siblings. He had no seatbelt on. He didn't make it.

I didn't know what to do, didn't know what to say. I took it in for a moment, holding back tears. "What do I do?"

"Nothing," she replied. "We'll send a letter home with your students, but you are not to talk with them about it."

I was heartbroken. I had never experienced death so close to me. I had lost distant relatives before, but this little guy, I had seen every day. I'd never expected to lose him. I knew his expressions of delight and of mischief. I could predict when he'd get bored with me, and I knew what he would run to each day on the playground. He was filled with life and shared that life with everyone. The grief that I was feeling during this time was multiplied because I could not talk about it with my students. My year was supposed to go on as if nothing had happened, as if no one was taken from us too soon.

A few days passed, and when I attended his funeral, I thought fondly of him. What a little stinker he was. He loved getting my attention, but he loved entertaining his peers even more. The only joy I could cling to was that the Friday before his passing, I had rewarded him for his self-control that week. He'd beamed with pride as he celebrated with the others who had been good decision makers. And then he was gone.

I'll never forget the day I decided I had to get out. I was driving home from work and listening to a Christian radio station, which wasn't my norm. A Casting Crowns song came on: "Who Am I." It talks about life being a quickly fading flower, a vapor in the wind. I had just stared at the smallest casket I had ever seen, an itty bitty child inside. If my life was a vapor, I could not go on living the way I was. In that moment, I decided to follow God's prompting and make a new start. I don't know that I would have given credit to the Holy Spirit at that time, but today I have no other answer.

Because I was close to my family and respected my parents (and because they had already made it clear that if I ever wanted to move far away, they would take it as a personal insult), I created a list of ten cities that piqued my interest. I'd seen enough corn and cows for a while, but I wanted my parents' input about my next stop in this quickly fading life. The cities I chose were relatively large, comprised of places I had seen on TV or that I had read about in books.

My parents took one look and said, "Atlanta." My older sister and her husband lived in a suburb outside the city, so Mom and Dad found comfort in knowing I'd have a relative nearby. I was ecstatic—I had a plan, and I knew where I was going. I had considered moving across the country before, but had never followed through. This time would be different. I couldn't explain the propelling force of faith that was carrying me forward, but God was all over it.

I got my resume together, sent out emails, and landed an interview—never mind that it was the end of the school year. I was ready for the change, but it was a bittersweet time for me. After all, the longest I had ever been away from my family was a week every year for church camp after we became regular church attenders, and that was only a forty-five-minute drive.

God captured me in this move in more ways than one. I had to trust Him, but I wasn't yet giving Him the credit He deserved for orchestrating the change. It wasn't until I was in Atlanta and settled in with my sister that I realized the real reason for my move. God picked me up, carried me away, and gave me a front-row seat to His will for my life. I realized that the real reason for my move was to wake me up from my wayward slumber, teaching me how to be a true follower of Christ.

I made it to my interview twenty minutes late. No one told me that every street name in Alpharetta changes at least once. Google was not yet a thing, so I didn't have their version of Maps that I now hold near and dear. Instead, I had a paper map that led me to a cul-de-sac with no school to be found. Despite my late arrival, however, I was offered a position to teach fourth grade in what would become my favorite school of my teaching career. It was the best place for me at the time, and God knew.

I recall the next scene as if it happened yesterday. My sister and I were going shopping, out for some quality girl time. We were headed down the suburban main street to the mall when traffic came to a complete stop. In disbelief I asked, "Why on earth is traffic stopped here on a Sunday?"

She replied, "There's a big church back there. I forgot. It's like this every Sunday."

Leave it to our God to use a shopping trip to introduce me to my new church home. I was intrigued. I told my sister I was going to check it out, and invited her to come along if she wanted. I figured if the church was good enough to stop traffic, it was a must-see for this new Georgia peach. I went the next Sunday and every Sunday after.

My real, personal relationship with Jesus began when I stepped into that church. Though I had accepted the gift of salvation years before, I found a fresh start in this place. Since my childhood baptism, I had not lived a life aligned with Christ. I had taken what I wanted out of the Bible and left the rest. Now, walking into my new church, I felt comfort, security, and new life. I felt God say, "You are home. You will be changed here."

It was a life-giving church. I'd never experienced services like these before. God used every element to woo me into a growing relationship with Him. That was the church's mission statement, and it stayed true to it. The church exists to lead people into a growing relationship with Jesus Christ. They were surely leading me.

I was apprehensive about getting involved in church by myself, but that was exactly what I needed. In fact, it was there that the title of this book came to me, *A Seamless Life*, because everything our heavenly Father offers us is just that— seamless. He intricately designs our entire lives and all our experiences with each of us in mind. He knows our every need and the individual desires of our hearts. He fits us together smoothly and perfectly, according to His seamless will. We just have to lean in and trust that everything will happen exactly as it's supposed to.

If you are like I was, in a place where God is calling you to something more, today is your day! God loves you like crazy, just as you are. He has seen you, loved you, and carried you all along. God's goodness and grace have protected you along the winding roads of life.

Maybe you've been walking with God a long time, but you know something is missing. Maybe your relationship with God has grown stale, and you're looking for that seamless plan He's said He has for you. Or maybe you are brand new to this. You probably have more questions than answers.

Everyone has been there. Let this be your beginning.

No matter where you are in your walk with the Lord, ask yourself the following questions. Find wisdom in what the Bible has to say, and pray along with me. I am praying for you, and I know God can and will use all things for His good and His glory.

Study Questions

1. What is the story of your beginning?
2. When did you first learn about God? Who or what would you credit with that introduction?
3. How has learning about God impacted your life?

Encouragement

> For everything there is a season, a time for every activity under heaven. (Ecclesiastes 3:1)

In the beginning the Word already existed. The Word was with God, and the Word was God. (John 1:1)

You will know the truth, and the truth will set you free. (John 8:32)

Prayer

Dear Lord, thank You for each precious reader You have led here. Please bless their lives and give them a renewed sense of connection with You. I pray we would all think back on the beginnings of our lives and thank You for the circumstances surrounding the relationship we have with You. Please use each of us to share Your love with the world. Every believer began somewhere, and You have placed us on our paths to reach others.

For those who do not know You, Lord, I pray that this book would spark their curiosity and interest in Your love and Your ways. Please bring other believers into their lives and let them find connection on their spiritual journey.

We love You and honor You this day and always. In Jesus's name, amen.

_____

_____

_____

_____

_____

_____

_____

_____

_____

_____

_____

_____

_____

CHAPTER TWO

SEAMLESS TRUST

May your will be done.

Matthew 6:10

GOD'S WILL IS seamless. You just have to lean in and trust that everything will happen exactly as it is supposed to.

The first time I heard about the will of God was when I read about Jesus in the garden of Gethsemane: "Yet I want your will to be done, not mine" (Luke 22:42). Growing up, I heard about God's will, sometimes over and over again, but it did not sink in deep until much later in life. I'm sure if you had a religious upbringing and have remained in church, this happened to you too.

"God's will" is not difficult to define. It's God's plan for your life. Despite the simple definition, however, navigating that plan can be challenging. If you are a believer in Christ and are pursuing a relationship with Him, you are in God's will. This thought both thrills and puzzles me at the same time. If you are an unbeliever, God also has a plan for you, but you might not have recognized it yet. We're here for a reason, whether we believe it or not. God has a purpose for each and every life. And that is His will—the reason you and I are here.

There have been times when I've had to make significant decisions, and loving people have prayed over me that I would pursue God's will—and I thought I was. But sometimes, if we look closely, we'll see that we're really pursuing our own desires, not His.

The amazing thing about our God is that He has grace for each of us. The sometimes dangerous thing about ourselves is that we can use that grace to "make friends" with our sin and thereby justify our actions. Christians walk a fine line of grace. God's will is accompanied by His grace for us. We often don't see the threads of grace God weaves into our lives until it's time for us to experience truth.

God always gives us the right amount of grace. He loves us and knows all our successes and failures. He knows what we delight in and what we struggle with. None of us is perfect, so we need Him to help us live with our imperfections. And He loves us enough to search for us when we're lost.

As Matthew 18:12 states, "If a man has a hundred sheep and one of them wanders away, what will he do? Won't he leave the ninety-nine others on the hills and go out to search for the one that is lost?" Yes, God will search for you, but you must be open and receptive to His call on your life.

God's will is good, pleasing, and perfect. The Bible tells us so. The trouble is, sometimes we can't see it. Our circumstances confuse us, so we dwell on "finding God's will." But if you're walking with Him, you're already in it. What does that mean? It depends on you.

If you do not know Him, I pray you will pursue that relationship, no matter the cost. It is the only relationship that will bring you true and lasting joy, peace, and comfort. To begin your walk with God, all you have to do is pray. Let Him know you're curious and interested to learn more about Him. He gives the invitation to all people. Psalm 27:11 is a request for more: "Teach me how to live, O Lord. Lead me along the right path, for my enemies are waiting for me."

Because of what Christ has done for us, we must not spend the rest of our lives chasing our own desires. Instead, we must press forward to do the will of God (1 Peter 4:2). We can ask God daily to reveal His will, but when vital decisions are necessary, we must pray specifically that He would unfold His will before us.

I remember a pivotal time in my life, when I was at a crossroads. I had an incredible job with a good salary, benefits, plenty of vacation time, and coworkers I loved. Simultaneously, I felt a pull to something new. I didn't know what that was at the time, so I had to pray for God's will to show up. I sensed that He wanted me to look for a new job, but I was perfectly happy where I was. So I prayed for this thought to go away or for doors to open.

Doors did open, and I applied for something new. Before that deal was sealed, I had to notify my current boss that I was not going to sign a contract for the upcoming year. Lots of people in my life thought I was crazy. Why would I give up my income, benefits, vacation, and amazing coworkers on a whim? It wasn't a whim to me. I had prayed, I felt God's peace, and I knew I was moving in the right direction. Although it may have been scary for some to watch, it was exactly what I needed.

Another time to pray for God's will is during conflict. No one is immune to conflict. The flesh we walk around in makes us prone to disagreement and misunderstanding. God can help with that. Proverbs 3:5 tells us not to depend on our own understanding. When tension is in the air, ask God to carry you and help you discern His will. I promise, it will make all the difference.

When you devote your whole life to Christ, you love and give out of a place of peace and joy. You might find yourself making radical life changes because the old life doesn't fit the new belief, or maybe your established traditions and religious practices will bring you to that centered place. If you seek God's will with all your heart, soul, and mind, you will be changed.

Your life and the way you live in God's will doesn't have to look like anyone else's. While your core values will line up with the teachings of Jesus, that can look different for you than it does for those around you. Hear me loud and clear, though. *Do not use a personal relationship with Christ as an excuse to act however you want, whenever you want, for whatever reason you want.* That does not represent God well, and it isn't in line with what the Bible instructs us to do as Christians.

Let me stop preaching for a moment to share some personal failure. I'll tell you, I'm on the road with my heavenly Father, but I have many shortcomings. As I wrote this chapter, the Holy Spirit brought to my mind my behavior in the workplace.

Prior to my leap of faith into this writing adventure, I taught elementary school for fifteen years. I also traveled for work as an educational consultant. In this role, I was contracted to work in schools across the country, but only for a week at a time. I would fly in on Sunday night, work onsite at the school Monday through Friday, and fly out again Friday night. When I married and had my first child, I decided it was time to stop earning frequent flier miles and return to the classroom.

In the daily grind, I can admit, I wasn't the best example of Christ. I was, and still am, a passionate educator with strong beliefs about the education all children deserve. My strong emotions caused me to be a poor representative of Jesus on several occasions. I have allowed my ego to prevent me from loving others, and through that, I failed many people. I failed myself. And I failed to carry out the real job God had entrusted me to do—to love Him and to love others.

Inside those many classrooms, I energetically taught my students the best I could. The classroom was my happy place; there I could do my job with the little people in my life. But outside the classroom, I walked away from coworkers, rolling my eyes. Often, my response or reaction to adults felt like an out-of-body experience. Afterward, I would look back and ask myself, "Why in the world would I say that? Why would I want to hurt them?"

I'm not proud of this, but now that I have confessed my sins to God and all of you, I can move on with life.

Was I in God's will? I was in that workplace and pursuing my relationship with Christ, but as a child of God, I was not acting as I should. I was being a hypocrite. Yet God's will was still being done. I can clearly see God's hand in relationships built or lessons learned at every school in my journey. No, I didn't always represent Him well, but God knew exactly how I would act, and He loved me anyway. Despite my failures, Romans 8:28 assures me that, "God causes everything to work together for the good of those who love God and are called according to his purpose for them."

In Christ, there is room for failure. He died so the imperfect could live freely. The beautiful part of failure is that we can say, "I realize the wrongdoing in my life, and I want to make some changes." We can't do that by ourselves. We might try, but we will succeed more seamlessly with the help of our God. This is called repentance, by the way. Repentance is seeing an error in your ways and making a decision to let Christ lead you into a better future.

God's will is exciting. The road can be dusty, but the journey is beautiful. I pray that we all get to know Him and live out His love for each of us and for all people. In Jesus's name, so be it. Amen.

Study Questions

1. Are you pursuing God's will for your life? How so?
2. Has God's grace changed you? If so, how?
3. In what one area of your life do you most need to focus on following God's will?

Encouragement

> Then Jesus explained: "My nourishment comes from doing the will of God, who sent me, and from finishing his work." (John 4:34)

He is so rich in kindness and grace that he purchased our freedom with the blood of his Son and forgave our sins. (Ephesians 1:7)

You won't spend the rest of your lives chasing your own desires, but you will be anxious to do the will of God. (1 Peter 4:2)

Prayer

Father, may Your will be done. We seek You for wisdom and discernment to know our next steps. Meet us where we are and lead us into Your will. Thank You for Your grace. Thank You for delivering us from our sin.

Help us to accept Your gift of grace and live a life of freedom, so we can lead others to You. In Christ's name we pray, amen.

CHAPTER THREE

SEAMLESS SURRENDER

I have been crucified with Christ; and it is no longer I who live, but Christ lives in me; and the life which I now live in the flesh I live by faith in the Son of God, who loved me and gave Himself up for me.

Galatians 2:20 NASB

WE SEE GOD'S hand in the seamlessness of the seasons of life: birth, childhood, single life, married life, and perhaps beyond. If you are unmarried, either you've decided to go with just the first three, or you are awaiting the last. Maybe you have an additional chapter of living alone as a divorcee or widower. I pray you find peace where you are on the journey.

My life as a single woman was tremendous but frivolous, all at the same time. I took much for granted. I followed any and every mission opportunity I felt called to, overplanning my weekends with whatever I wanted to do, underplanning and watching sappy movies on the couch all weekend long. When you're single, you don't have as many concerns as a married person does. Sure, there are family concerns, work concerns, and health concerns. The single life isn't all whipped cream and cherries. However, a single woman can spend her time participating in and concerning herself with whatever she wants.

In my single life, I worried about many things. *What if I don't meet him? I want to be a mother. Am I in the right career? Should I feel more fulfilled than this? Are my friends real friends or just people who hang out with me when they're bored?* I now see that all these worries were self-centered, not God-centered. Deep down, I knew I didn't need to worry. I knew God would provide all my needs. I just needed some proof, you know? But I didn't need self-centered worry; I needed God-centered faith.

My first few single years were a mess. I dumped my high school/college sweetheart for no reason apparent to others. He had proposed; I had accepted—he wasn't just a boyfriend anymore. He was an amazing person with a wonderful family, and my own family love-love-*loved* him. It's hard to do the right yet difficult thing when no one understands what you're doing. The only reason I broke our engagement was because God prompted me to do so. During those years, I wasn't as close to God as I am now, but the Holy Spirit still worked in me. If there was hope for me then, there surely is for you.

The next few years weren't much different. New city, new long-term boyfriend. He was another amazing person with a wonderful family. This time, his family lived several states away, so my life wasn't as intertwined with them as it had been with my first fiancé. And this time, we didn't have a formal engagement, but we did talk about marriage, long-term living, and shared life goals. After a few years of ups and downs, I felt God calling me to end that relationship too. Although it was difficult, I didn't want to miss God's best for me. I knew deep down that this relationship wasn't it.

Despite all my wandering and wondering in relationships, God instilled in me a list of perfect-for-me qualities in a man. I became friends with a lovely group of ladies, and they encouraged me to write down the list. Looking back, that may have been good advice, but it was also preposterous. I saw it as an exercise to define what I was looking for. God had other plans.

I remember a sermon our pastor preached to singles in our church. I still pass on the principle to my single friends: Instead of defining the man you want, become the woman your ideal man is looking for. Focus on becoming the person you want to be when you meet the man of your dreams. *Ah ha!* Mindset shift. Instead of looking for "him," I had to get to work on me.

My checklist for my man soon became my checklist for my mirror. But not my physical mirror—an inner one. An ordinary mirror reflects the outward appearance, but I needed a deep, soul-searching variety, one that would shine light on my flaws and show me the qualities other people see in me. The Holy Spirit was the mirror I needed.

The Holy Spirit is also like a microscope. When you put your faith and trust in Jesus, proclaim He is Lord of all, and accept all He offers and requires, the Holy Spirit shows up. If you welcome and pursue that relationship, God will reveal issues for you to work on. Once you've made progress, the lens will focus on something new. The Holy Spirit is the game changer in living a godly life. His influence makes all the difference.

Armed with new information, I decided to stop dating altogether. I remember a journal entry from that time: "If you love God so much, why do you flirt with the world?" Ouch. I admit I enjoyed male attention. I'm not proud of it, but it was true. I didn't want a new relationship, but I didn't mind going on a date and casually getting to know someone new.

But God . . .

He required full attention. In order to make it to the promise of the lasting love I knew existed for me, I had to give up the attention of the casual callers. God knew the desires of my heart, and I knew one of two things would happen. Either He would fulfill the desires of my heart more abundantly than I had ever dreamed, or He would change those desires. I was fine with either one.

So I surrendered to God's way. I stopped answering calls. I didn't go on any more dates. Not everyone will take this route, because most people handle the dating process just fine. But some of us can find ourselves addicted to dating, and in that case, it's best to keep away from it until God shows us a wiser way.

I had just turned thirty as I began my dating break. Society's dark clouds of relationship expectations still hung over me. Historically, whenever I'd expressed interest in a man, my friends and family always asked, "Do you think he's the one?" For me to stop paying attention to men was outrageous to their mainstream minds. I didn't care.

I spent several months in deliberate isolation, then one day, a new man entered the picture. He was not on my dating radar, but God used the logistics of our meeting to help take down my walls. We lived in different states when we began our relationship. I didn't mind because I needed to get to know him over the phone before I could know whether he was God's answer to my prayers. Nine months after our initial meeting, Taylor asked my father for permission to propose. A few months after that, he did. Five months later, we had the best wedding I've ever seen.

Point #1: With God, all things are possible.

Point #2: When you trust God with all, He works in all.

Point #3: When you know, you know.

And what about my list? My husband exceeded my expectations. After he proposed, I scrawled a check mark across each box on that list. But, like us all, he has a past, so I also had to check a few boxes on my never-date-this-guy list. To help me learn how wonderful our Creator made my love, He suspended my judgment for a period of time. I did not judge Taylor's past or present habits during our season of dating. This was a different scenario for me, because before I met Taylor, my lists were quite extensive, and I stuck to them. With Taylor, it was like God was reminding me to address the plank in my own eye before examining the speck in his.

I learned that if God can overlook my flaws and bring beauty from ashes, then I could overlook Taylor's flaws too. (Please understand, I am not recommending you walk down the aisle with a criminal, an abuser, or anyone who is deep in sin and doesn't want to get out.) We all are imperfect beings in a messed-up world, but amid all the imperfection, God restores beauty and creates masterpieces on a daily basis. He makes all things new.

Taylor and I got married after a whirlwind romance. Some people said, "You don't know each other at all!" They were right. We had a lot to learn about the servanthood of marriage.

Of course, Taylor and I had our own stories of past mistakes, and they were very different, but now we were joining forces and would succeed or fail together. We completed premarital counseling, which I recommend for everyone. It will equip you with information about topics you will likely never discuss over dinner or on a date.

We came away from counseling with at least one major lesson. In order for marriage to work, we had to be a team. Mark 10:8 lets us know that when we get married, we are no longer two, but one. We felt so strongly about this concept, we had "One" engraved inside our wedding bands.

I wish I could say that, from our wedding day forward, we have agreed on everything and life has been peachy. Not so. The Bible has many applications for daily life. Sometimes when we read a Scripture, we feel empowered because we're on the same wavelength. "Yes, we will be one. We can do this together!" Other times, we read the same Scripture and feel convicted. "I know, I know. We are no longer two, but one."

Marriage is not always easy, but it works if we plan for success together. Over the years, I've heard lots of marital wisdom from several pastors. They are all married. They are all respected and spoken of highly by their wives. They all agree that marriage is best when two servants are in love, walking with the Lord and serving one another.

Just as I had to surrender to God's plan for my relationships, I have to surrender to His plan in my marriage. I believe I have the best husband for me on the planet, but we do not see eye to eye on all things.

I need God's wisdom in navigating my marriage. I must surrender to God's will within my preferences. This has been a huge awakening for me. I lived on my own for ten years before I got married. I'm not picky, but I am preferential.

Through my marriage, God has shown me that some of my former preferences were fickle. When my husband unloads the dishwasher for me, it doesn't matter which forks he puts in which compartment. He has helped me simply by unloading the dishes. It took me almost seven years to surrender this preference. How silly of me.

Similarly, my desire to have all the laundry put into the proper closets immediately after folding is ridiculous. At some point soon, our children will be old enough to pick up their own baskets and take care of their own clothes. For now, I will choose to be grateful that my man took the laundry out of the dryer to begin with.

When we travel, I prefer to go the most efficient way possible. Taylor loves the scenic route. I admire that about him. He slows me down and helps me enjoy the beauty around us. I'm just trying to get there, but he worships along the way. Surrendering your preferences isn't always an internal pep talk with no reward. Sometimes you gain a better understanding of who God is in the process.

Another place I have had to lay down my own will and seek God's will in my marriage is in our schedule and use of time. Coordinating two schedules has been a challenge. At first, I had my plans, and Taylor had his. When you get married, however, those two schedules must mesh into one.

During our first year of marriage, Taylor and I shared a car. When I went somewhere, so did he and vice versa. If you want to get to know someone on a deeper level, do this. If not, two cars for two people is my suggestion.

The first year, the scheduling department was pretty easy. But the next year—whoa, did that throw everything off! Everything changed in our lives. We moved across the country, Taylor started graduate school, and we had a new baby. We bought another car.

The schedule was difficult. It was a point of conflict in our house as we tried to balance work, school, childcare, church activities, and family get-togethers. I don't know what happens at your house, but we were caught in a constant rundown of the day's activities and who was going to be home when.

I started resenting this lifestyle. I didn't feel as if Taylor and I were on the same team, and I had a harder time communicating with him when I felt that way. I had to surrender to God's will in this. I had to accept the fact that our busy schedules were current and future blessings. Nevertheless, we had to work something out so we could feel like one instead of two again.

Late at night or on weekends, we discussed our schedules and tried to come up with solutions, but the conversation usually ended in disagreement. It became uncomfortable. Finally, Taylor asked if we could try sharing an electronic calendar. That was a brilliant solution. Not only did this new method allow us to schedule events that included the whole family, but we could add individual events for which we wanted prayer. From the first day with our new calendar, God has blessed our marriage and family with the peace of knowing what is going on from day to day.

Taylor and I often reevaluate our calendars to make sure they line up with our values. If we are overscheduling, we scale it back a bit. When we surrender to God's will in our marriage and join forces as one, all things are possible, and we can overcome our issues peacefully.

Finally, I have learned to surrender to God's will in my marriage by parenting God's way. As new parents, we didn't know what we were doing. Does anyone? Very quickly, we learned that new parents try everything they've heard about, then they see what works.

That was fine until our daughter turned two. I didn't know how to handle a newborn, but we got through it. I kept up with all her milestones and shared appropriately with family and friends. Then Emerson started talking, and I was at a loss. Oh, and did I mention that when she was nine months old, we found out a little boy was on the way? At the same moment my two-year-old daughter was supposed to turn terrible, I had a three-month-old boy in my lap at all times. It was rough but definitely sweet.

As the children got older, Taylor and I started to pull out parenting tricks from our own pasts. We didn't talk about these parenting methods until we started using them. In my opinion, his tactics were too strong for toddlers, and he considered mine too weak. Our disagreement on parenting methods went on for more than a year.

We were back at our starting point: if we two had become one, why did we feel so separate?

I now know the answer: Satan wants to wreck marriages. He wants to destroy the relationships between husbands and wives and between parents and children. We must claim our marriages and parenting in the name of Jesus.

We knew our imbalanced parenting wasn't working, so we sought help and eventually started a small group for other struggling parents. You might laugh about that, but when we need a good dose of wisdom and renewed vision, we must surrender, pray, and move forward with the next right step God gives us. He called us to lead a small group for other parents who didn't have it all figured out and wanted to work through the challenges together.

God used that time and those friendships to teach Taylor and me to connect with Him first in all things. We learned to establish our expectations as one. This is a constant effort, and I'm sure we have many more refining experiences to walk through. However, when we put God first and seek His will as parents, our perspectives change for the better.

Parenting is the most challenging and rewarding responsibility God gives us. With that responsibility, why would we not want to do it His way?

Surrendering to God's will looks different depending on the changing seasons of our lives. If we put Him first, seek His wisdom, and act according to the calling He puts on our hearts, we will live our best life. John 12:25 says, "Those who love their life in this world will lose it. Those who care nothing for their life in this world will keep it for eternity." We must surrender our lives to find them in Christ.

Study Questions

1. Have you had to surrender something important in order to follow Christ? If so, what was it, and how did you feel throughout the process?

2. What do you find most difficult about surrendering to God's will?

3. Sometimes in relationships, we must surrender our expectations in order to follow the will of God. Can you think of a time when you had to modify expectations so you could be more like Christ? Please share.

Encouragement

> Joyful are people of integrity, who follow the instructions of the LORD. Joyful are those who obey his laws and search for him with all their hearts. They do not compromise with evil, and they walk only in his paths. You have charged us to keep your commandments carefully. Oh, that my actions would consistently reflect your decrees! Then I will not be ashamed when I compare my life with your commands. As I learn your righteous regulations, I will thank you by living as I should! I will obey your decrees. Please don't give up on me! (Psalm 119:1–8)

Prayer

Dear God, we seek You. We so desire to surrender our own will for Yours. Please help us lay down all that holds us back from the truest following of our lives. Break strongholds and renew our faith and strength. We surrender all that has gotten in the way of knowing You.

I pray a special prayer for those who are far from You, Lord. We know that following Your will is the best way to live. Please help us shine Your light and be examples of Your love and grace to others, so they might pursue Your will too.

We join together in prayer. In Jesus's name, amen.

Chapter Four

SEAMLESS NURTURING

You will find Him if you seek Him with all your heart and with all your soul.

Deuteronomy 4:29 NKJV

MY BEST FRIENDS have positively impacted my life in ways I'm sure I don't realize and haven't credited to them. Similarly, we sometimes fail to recognize God's dealings with us. This is the seamless nurturing of our God. He trains us and provides for us, though we may not recognize His work at the time.

Spending time in God's presence and in the company of godly friends is easy to write about but difficult to do. Being with God and my friends is not the hard part. The hard part is prioritizing my life around what matters most: my relationship with Christ and the people He has blessed me with.

The Bible says, "As iron sharpens iron, so a friend sharpens a friend" (Proverbs 27:17). I have an array of friendships—very close friends, close friends, friends who knew me before I knew Jesus, and acquaintances. You likely have some of the same categories. I will break down the reasons all those relationships are important to me.

Finding very close friends is a treasure. I have only a handful, but I can share anything with them, and they still love me. Similarly, nothing they share with me will change my love for them. I communicate with my very close friends regularly. I see them as often as possible. They are all at the same stage of life as I am, so we relate on several levels—as Christians, as wives, as mothers.

Close friends are precious too. I have several close friends I frequently check on through calls, texts, coffee dates, and prayers. Close friends are gifts from God. They make you feel comfortable in a crowded room and listen any time you want to talk.

Even though I've attended church for many years, I have a group of friends who knew me way back when I didn't "get it" with Jesus. These friends are true, and I love them for the history and stories we share. I'm happy to see them from time to time and love catching up. Friends who knew you before you knew Jesus are wonderful reminders that we all need saving. Only one Savior can bring you out of the pit of despair and put your feet on solid ground—ground that can make you quite unrecognizable to the ones who knew you in the pit.

Acquaintances are all around us. You see the same people going into church, the grocery store, and your children's schools. You are acquainted but haven't taken a step to create a friendship. Maybe there's hope for a future friendship, but right now, you merely cross paths every now and then.

I once thought I should become the best of friends with every Christian I met. That is simply not the case. Not everyone is meant to be a close friend, but no matter a person's role in your life, Jesus died for them. Each person you see is as important to God as you are. Finding your right relationship with everyone God puts in your path can be a daunting task. With prayer and discernment, you can nurture relationships and give them their proper position in your life.

In a church leadership training session, I completed an exercise that required each participant to draw two concentric circles on a piece of paper. In the inner circle, we wrote the names of people who had the greatest influence in our lives: our very close friends and family members. In the next circle, we wrote the names of friends and family members who were not in the inner circle. Outside both circles, we wrote any other names that came to mind.

We did this exercise to show God's influence through people. Not only does God use those in your inner circle in your life, but He also uses you in theirs. He uses those in the larger circle in your life the same way—and uses you in theirs. He uses you to love and minister to those outside the circles.

Relationships are opportunities to share God's love in action. I recently went through a StrengthsFinder group with a few ladies from my church. StrengthsFinder focuses on the fact that God bestows different strengths on each of us. In order to live in your strengths, you must know what they are. Sure, you can wander around in life, thinking you know what you're good at, but taking time to focus on what He created you to do is invaluable.

I was surprised to learn that my top strength was being a Realtor. I took one look and thought, "Oh, my! I'm not in real estate." But as I looked at the characteristics of that strength, I went back and read the title again—correctly.

Of course. I *am* a relator. I relate. That's what I do.

I've been relating forever. As long as I can remember, I've sought out solid friendships. As times change and the world becomes more tech-savvy, I am increasingly frustrated with our lack of real relationships. I value a phone call or, even better, sharing coffee or lunch with a friend. I thrive in friendships of mutual investment.

In our current screen-obsessed culture, cultivating meaningful relationships takes a lot of effort, but it's well worth it. I've tried to make a habit of scrolling through my contacts list and calling or texting someone I haven't spoken to in a while. Sure, I'm not going to call to chitchat with my exterminator or my dentist, but my friends enjoy a check-in every once in a while.

I challenge you to look through your phone's contact list as soon as you get a chance. Give it a quick evaluation. When is the last time you saw, talked to, or sent a text to each person?

The people in your inner circle definitely have the most influence on you. Who are they? Do they live the way you want to live? Do you need to make adjustments or have a difficult conversation to put those relationships in the proper place in your life?

Because of our ever-changing methods of communication and increasing lack of presence in relationships, the way we relate to God has changed as well. I can't speak for anyone else, but the tech culture has me in a hurry all the time. It's not that I'm an impatient person; I can be very patient. But with immediate access to any and all information (true and false), I have rushed the most valuable thing to me: relationships.

God is a patient God. He will wait on us. But while He waits, we miss out. Devoted time in His presence opens up godly wisdom, courage, clarity, discernment—gifts we do not receive if we do not spend time with Him. This world has come up with crafty, faulty replacements for God's gifts: foolish advice, liquid/online courage, horoscopes, and more. I can call them out because they've all tricked me at one time or another. But after time alone with Jesus, we experience grace and can extend it to those who are lost.

While God is patient with us, we must remember that we are called to wait on Him, as well. Hosea 6:3 says, "Oh, that we might know the Lord! Let us press on to know him. He will respond to us as surely as the arrival of dawn or the coming of rains in early spring." He will respond, but sometimes we have to wait too.

I can now speak from a place of desiring a deeper relationship with the Lord, but I also know He works in me with the time I have. It can be frustrating to want more time with God, especially when I realize I don't prioritize Him as I should. I'm in a season of transition, and Satan tries to throw off my spiritual disciplines by distracting me during my quiet time.

As a Christian, I value quiet, alone time with my Bible and whatever truth the Holy Spirit brings to light. Because I've always been a writer in some sense, I keep a journal (or several) with me when I pray.

As a wife, I've worked hard with my husband to develop a strategy for learning together from the Lord. Right now, that means getting up an hour earlier than the kids so we can read a devotional. We like to vary this time. We cannot stick to one devotional book, or maybe we just haven't found one that works for us. Sometimes we watch online sermons together or listen to podcasts while taking care of other tasks. And there is always prayer. When we're on the same page of the Bible, we are more in sync in all areas of life.

As a mother, I constantly ask God for renewed strength and patience. I pray often that my children will see me as a ray of light and not a thundercloud of darkness. My kids are little, so we read Bible stories, sing praise songs, and pray together. This brings me closer to God, and it instills a desire for relationship with Him into my children.

As a friend, I pray over all requests sent my way. I ask the Lord to show me which members of my inner and outer circles need prayer. I celebrate my friends' successes, and I'm there for them in the difficult times too.

I'm not perfect in any of the above roles, but every morning when I get up, I purpose in my heart to put God first in all these areas. This makes a delightful difference in my heart and, I hope, in my actions.

The Bible tells us to "not get tired of doing good. At just the right time, we will reap a harvest of blessing if we don't give up" (Galatians 6:9). It encourages us to consistently strive for God's best, even when we can't accomplish what we set out to do.

I always come back to Paul's words in Romans 7:19: "I want to do what is good, but I don't. I don't want to do what is wrong, but I do it anyway." Paul is ticked at himself for not being able to carry out the very thing he knows he wants to do. And he's equally upset that he continues doing things he doesn't want to do. Isn't this all of us? Maybe not, but if you don't run into this, please contact me directly. I need your help with this one!

Everything comes down to the time we spend in His presence. We can wake up one day and fail to acknowledge our Savior. We can wake up the next and spend all day praising Him. Or we can be real with the daily struggle of carrying out the greatest commandment and know our only help is the time we spend renewing our minds with the promises and assignments God has given us.

When we neglect our Savior, both our hearts and our relationships suffer. As someone who wants to walk with God, you have to know what you need to make that walk a daily choice. If you have to get up an hour earlier to start your mind and day off right with God, do it. If you need to stockpile devotionals so you never run out of content, start shopping. Maybe you need to download an app that will support your walk with the Lord. Our disciplines may look different, but one thing is the same: Life is best lived when pursuing God. Make it happen.

I get annoyed when I hear a message telling me one size fits all in the daily devotions department. The way you interact with God is probably different than most people you meet, and that is okay.

Comparisons of worship, quiet time, connection, mission work, and the like—these are not godly praise. If you're caught up in comparing your method of serving God to that of others, please lay that burden down. My husband taught this lesson to me, and he doesn't even know it.

One day on a walk through our neighborhood, I caught my husband staring up into the trees, a smile on his face. He was worshiping God through his love of nature. Another time, on a hike in a nearby park, I was looking for the fastest route back to the car. Taylor took the longest way possible, just to see more of God's creation. When we drive through mountains or the country, I have to make sure I'm behind the wheel. Taylor gets distracted by God's beauty. We all should be more like him.

When we met, I was still in my regimented-religion phase. I had a routine worked out with God, and that was how I drew close to Him. I tried to push that plan onto everyone around me. If their way was different, I saw it as inferior. What a sin! Spiritual disciplines—prayer, studying God's Word, fellowship with other believers, and such—only assist us in growing closer to God. If our focus is on the routine of our disciplines and not the purpose, we've missed the point.

However and whenever you can spend time drawing near to God, you will be richly rewarded. He is pleased when we seek Him. Period. We can seek Him in many ways. When I first started dating Taylor and we spent time outside, I was intrigued by his curiosity about and joy in nature. Standing in awe of God's wonder was not my spiritual path, but Taylor gave reverence to God and thanked Him for all He had made. I had to learn that finding wonder in God's creation is an act of worship all by itself. Praising God and being grateful for His creation is a way to show appreciation and thanksgiving.

My go-to method of experiencing the presence of God is to read the Bible. I grew up reading a version whose words I couldn't pronounce, much less understand. I suggest spending time in the Bible aisle of any bookstore to find a version of the Bible that fits you. You'll gain much more wisdom when you connect with the way God's truths are written. And those truths will change your life.

I lived a Christ-adjacent life before I became the Christ-follower I am now. I use the term "Christ-adjacent" because I was close to surrendering my will to Christ's, but right along the edge lived some things that were difficult for me to lay down. I was involved in Christian things. I wasn't opposed to attending church. I hung out with Christian friends at times. I prayed fairly regularly. I enjoyed all those things . . . well, mostly. Yet I thought the great big God, the One who made me and was up in heaven looking out for me, was too big to encounter for myself. I understood the crucifixion, but I didn't claim it personally. Until I finally bought my own Bible, for myself, by myself. A version I could understand. I remember standing in the Christian bookstore that day, thinking, *What an adult move this is!* Oh, how silly of me. God probably laughed out loud. He knew the power that day held. He unlocked godly wisdom for me that day.

No matter which way you get into His presence, once you are there, choose to stay there. You must continue to submit and surrender to God's will in order to stay there. No matter which vehicle you choose to travel cross-country in, if you keep moving, you will get there. Some vehicles take longer, some have a bumpier ride, and some might even break down a time or two, but the vehicle isn't the point. It's all about the destination. The journey is God's seamless story of love and grace for each of us.

Study Questions

1. Have you ever completed an activity like the one described

in this chapter: making concentric circles of your people? If not, I urge you to grab a piece of paper and draw two circles. Place the names of those closest to you in the middle and others in the appropriate place either in the next circle or around the edges. Then evaluate. Are you positively influenced by those in your inner circle? Are they positively influenced by you?

2. Do your relationships help you grow in your faith? If not, what needs to change?

3. Which version of the Bible is your favorite? If you don't have a favorite, make it a goal to find one.

Encouragement

The seeds of good deeds become a tree of life; a wise person wins friends. (Proverbs 11:30)

A friend is always loyal, and a brother is born to help in time of need. (Proverbs 17:17)

Surely righteous people are praising your name; the godly will live in your presence. (Psalm 140:13)

Prayer

Heavenly Father, we thank You for the friends You have given us to walk with in this life. We pray that You would bless our friendships, drawing us closer to You and to each other.

Lord, I pray for the relationships we're involved in that do not bring out the best in us. I pray we would be transparent enough to bring those relationships to You so You can show us how to navigate them.

I pray for everyone reading this right now, that You would bring godly relationships into their lives. I pray we would seek Your Word for wisdom and understanding.

Teach us Your ways as we live out our days. In Your Son's holy name, amen.

CHAPTER FIVE

SEAMLESS CONFIDENCE

We have the mind of Christ.

1 Corinthians 2:16

ONE HIGHLIGHT OF a growing relationship with Christ is developing confidence that His will is best for you. When you receive affirmation and confirmation from above, that's God sharing His fulfilled promises in tangible ways.

God affirms His will by answering prayers. Suppose you prayed for open doors in a new career. Then, out of nowhere, you receive new job postings in your inbox. This could be God affirming your request for doors to open. If you pray for health or healing and miraculous healing occurs, God has affirmed your trust in Him during uncertain times. You may not get the first job you pursue or enjoy perfect health for the rest of all time, but God is there to declare His presence in your life.

Likewise, God confirms His will by sending winks of approval—signs and signals that He is involved. During a time of uncertainty, He may use a song that gives you new assurance to follow Him. The Holy Spirit may give you a verse to ponder or a song of encouragement when you face a big decision. God is in the details of our lives, and He shows up to fulfill His promises. God uses everything—even circumstances that seem insignificant—to bring greater glory back to Himself.

Not long ago, my husband and I needed a new house. We moved back to the Midwest from the South, wanting to plant some roots. With the help of Craigslist, my parents' phones, and a virtual open house, we bought our first home together—a two-bedroom bungalow. Better than our previous rental properties, our little bungalow provided a permanence that was perfect for that time in our lives.

When we found out we were expecting our third baby, we knew it was time to go. Two bedrooms weren't enough anymore. We lived in a quaint community that enjoyed a sold-in-twenty-four-hours real-estate market. During our family walks around town, we kept our eyes open for the perfect new place. Many times, we said, "This is it! This house is just right for us." But every time we requested a showing, we found a sale was already pending. Bummer.

Lo and behold, God had other plans.

We were living on one income. My husband was almost done with graduate school, and the numbers we were working with were ridiculous. Our budget was so slim, we were sure we couldn't make a move that would result in a forever home. We were ready to move up, but we didn't think we could afford a house that would fit our family for the long haul.

After many failed attempts, we started thinking maybe we were jumping the gun on the house-buying plans. We were right. At my first ultrasound appointment, the technician informed us that the baby had stopped growing at nine and a half weeks. Words alone had never made me feel numb before that day.

It was a difficult time. We hadn't told many people that we were expecting. I was heartbroken, afraid, confused, and felt like a failure. I didn't know how to move on, yet I could feel the peace of God as I clung to my doctor's words: "When it happens this early, there is a reason." All I knew was that I didn't want to go through this again. I told my doctor that Taylor and I didn't want to have any more babies. But God had other plans.

This is about a house, right? Ah, yes, the house. After I came out of short-term depression, I kept an eye on the For Sale signs in the neighborhood. A couple of them sparked interest, but this time it was just for fun, not because we had to move. Our real-estate agent was patient and set up appointments to fit our schedule. A house around the corner had potential. It was charming, but the floor plan was off. As we looked around, I kept trying to fit the pieces together out loud. Then the Realtor said, "I have a new listing you may be interested in." That was all it took.

Her words hit me in a divine way. Crazy, I know, but true. Taylor and I told the agent to go ahead and set up an appointment to look at this one last house. Meanwhile, we went home, searched the listing, and found out the house was three times the size of ours and the price was way over our budget. We started laughing, but together said, "We'll go ahead and look at it anyway."

I'm a prayer warrior. I pray all the time. I pray for huge things and for small, insignificant things. It's how He created me. Just as parents find delight in our children's individual idiosyncrasies, I believe God laughs in delight at some of my prayers. I'm fine with that.

Before viewing the house, I remember praying, "God, if this is meant to be, even though it doesn't fit with our worldly comprehension, show me."

We walked into a house from the late eighties, expressed through wallpaper and color schemes. But when we looked beyond that, it was a gorgeous house.

We kept walking. Our kids ran through the house, and I could envision that happening for years to come.

We explored some more. Finally, we made it to the front room, where the only piece of furniture left in the house sat before us—a baby grand piano. To anyone else, this would probably be a meaningless detail, but to me, it was God. Ever since I was six years old, I've loved the piano and have played it by ear my whole life.

We kept looking. We found a detail that other potential buyers might have missed. Set into each doorknob on the first floor was a fleur-de-lis. My husband and I hadn't just moved up from the South; we moved up from New Orleans, where the fleur-de-lis is the official symbol. God was telling us we were home.

When we left that day, I knew we would live there. I didn't know how we would work out the details, but God did. We had some stressful days ahead, working through the sale of our house (to my mother, who still lives there today!), purchasing the new house, settling the inspection, the timing . . . but in everything, I felt the peace and presence of God. We knew we had no reason to worry, and we didn't. God took great care of us.

Not long after we moved in, I wasn't feeling like myself. I wasn't sleeping well, felt exhausted at all times, and started to notice the veins in my legs more than usual. The combination could mean only one thing. Two pregnancy tests later, I called my doctor once again. God had other plans, and that plan is calling, "Mama!" right now.

I have a hundred stories like this one. I have a hundred friends with a hundred more stories like this one. When you seek a relationship with Christ, He meets you right where you are. God affirms you by validating His will for your life. The Holy Spirit confirms His plans by giving you new assurance in the right direction.

When you walk with God, you'll see Him affirm and confirm your right steps and your missteps in other ways too. In 2 Timothy 3:16, we find that "all Scripture is inspired by God and is useful to teach us what is true and to make us realize what is wrong in our lives. It corrects us when we are wrong and teaches us to do what is right." When you read the Bible, God speaks through the words to give you His Word.

I have several versions of the Bible. I read them at different times for different reasons. One version stays beside my bed. I open it and read it like a novel. The Bible is filled with amazing stories of incredible victories, stories that give me confidence in our Lord and inspiration to take on my circumstances. I have another version of the Bible that I use for everyday studying. When I am working through a devotional or Bible study, it is my reference for all Scriptures. I also have a chronological Bible, so I can read of God's deliverance in the order in which it occurred.

No matter which version of the Bible you prefer, God will use His Word to confirm His will to you. You can pray about an issue and research it to find that God is right there with you in it.

Just a few months ago, I attended a ladies-only small group. The leader of the group prayed about the discussion topics and then used those topics to start the conversation. One night, the conversation didn't go as planned, and she didn't get back to the verse God had put on her heart to share that day.

As everyone got ready to leave, one lingering conversation allowed me to share my verse of the season, Isaiah 43:19: "I am about to do something new. See, I have already begun! Do you not see it?"

From across the room, I heard, "Shut up! Shut up! What did you just say?"

I repeated the verse I'd quoted often during this time in my life. The leader turned pages in her Bible and said, "That's the verse God gave me for this group tonight!"

God confirmed the promises of new beginnings through both of us by directing our attention to His Scripture.

God uses the people in your life to bring you truth, as well as the lessons and wisdom He wants you to have. The people He has placed around you can affirm your confidence. Proverbs 15:22 assures us that "many advisers bring success." God never intended for us to do life alone. He will use wise advisers to direct you in your walk with Him.

Taylor and I actively seek God's will each day—individually, as a couple, and as a family. God has not only given me the best husband but a wise adviser too. Whenever I head down the wrong path in thoughts or actions, Taylor sits with me and, with grace, leads me back to right believing or behaving. God will use your spouse to confirm His will for your life and you in theirs as well.

I touch more on this in the next chapter, but the Bible tells us that the Holy Spirit leads in all truth and lives within us (John 14:17). In order to receive confirmation from the Holy Spirit, however, we must quiet our worlds. Sometimes we receive blaring messages that are hard to ignore, no matter the surrounding noise, but just as often, we hear from the Holy Spirit when we devote time to listening. We receive words of wisdom and reassurance to continue on our current path or repent and head in a new direction.

Sometimes God will direct you to a time of fasting and prayer to give you confidence and shed light on His will for you. While the Bible discusses fasting in several places, the book of Daniel is probably the best known. In Daniel 9, you can discover why Daniel fasted. In a nutshell, he was praying and pleading for the people of Jerusalem. After devoted prayer and fasting, Daniel received insight and understanding from Gabriel, sent by God.

If you have never participated in a fast, let me tell you what it is not. A fast is not a fad diet. It's not a bandwagon of fasting groupies who all want to do the same fast at the same time. A fast is not a time to starve yourself and make a big deal about how much you cannot eat. It is also not a new, trendy weight-loss plan.

Fasting is an act of devotion to God. When we fast, we sacrifice the insignificant, which we consume without thinking, for the most significant Bread of Life. Fasting draws us closer to God. Study Daniel as an example. When we make a change in eating habits, we can pay more attention to all the ways God wants to speak to us during the fasting period.

Fasting and prayer go hand in hand because we need prayer when we do not eat. As you fast, every time you think of the food you are living without, pray and give thanks to God for all He has done and will do for you.

There are many types of fasts. Some restrict certain types of foods, some are based on the biblical diet, and others are liquid-only fasts. Pray first. God will give you discernment as to what is right for you. If you are a part of a local church, ask for more information there. If not, look into online resources, but don't believe everything you read.

My church starts the year with twenty-one days of fasting and prayer. The pastors encourage believers and attenders to pray about how God wants them to use the time, and they provide helpful resources for those with questions about different types of fasts.

I mentioned that a fast is not a bandwagon deal. Some may ask, "But if your whole church does this together, how is that not a bandwagon?" The purpose of a congregation-wide fast is to support, encourage, and pray for one another during the fasting period. As in Daniel's story, you will receive insight and understanding through the act of fasting.

Seamless confidence in Christ is a treasure. Matthew 7:7 encourages us to seek Him. When we do, we will find Him. Knock and He will answer. Ask and it will be given to you. And it will all bring glory to God.

Study Questions

1. Have you ever sensed God speaking right to you? What message did you receive?

2. Has God confirmed anything to you through someone or something else? Please share.

3. What do you know about fasting? Do you see a reason for pursuing a time of fasting and prayer in your own life?

Encouragement

O LORD, you have examined my heart and know everything about me. You know when I sit down or stand up. You know my thoughts even when I'm far away. You see me when I travel and when I rest at home. You know everything I do. You know what I am going to say even before I say it, LORD. You go before me and follow me. You place your hand of blessing on my head. Such knowledge is too wonderful for me, too great for me to understand! (Psalm 139:1–6)

Let us hold tightly without wavering to the hope we affirm, for God can be trusted to keep his promise. (Hebrews 10:23)

Prayer

Dear God, thank You for the ways You have made us. Thank You for the idiosyncrasies that make us who we are. Thank You for showing us how much You love and care for us.

Please continue to confirm Your will to us. Continue to let us know we're right where we should be when we're in Your will.

Guard our hearts and our minds from any diversion from Your path. We choose Your will and are grateful to feel Your closeness on our journeys.

In Jesus's name, amen.

Chapter Six

SEAMLESS SPIRITUALITY

But you shall receive power when the Holy Spirit has come upon you;
and you shall be witnesses to Me in Jerusalem, and in all Judea
and Samaria, and to the end of the earth.

Acts 1:8 NKJV

ONCE I REALIZED the power of the Holy Spirit, my life changed, and I never want to go back to living a powerless life. I used to sit in church and listen (or daydream and plan the rest of my day), but I never found it necessary to take notes. Now when I go to church, I have so many notes, I can't make sense of them all later. I want to share some of what my pastor has been teaching on the Holy Spirit, but instead of typing straight from my sermon notes, I'm going to start with my story: how I got to know the Holy Spirit.

Growing up, I had no idea who the Holy Spirit was or what He did. I knew He was part of the Holy Trinity, but I didn't know He could have an impact on my life. I sang hymns that used His name, but they didn't mean anything to me personally. It wasn't until the Holy Spirit began to play a part in my prayer life and journaling, that I recognized and gave Him credit.

My journals are filled with writing that isn't mine. I physically wrote the words, but I didn't conceive the thoughts. Journaling started as a hobby, the written expression of thoughts I didn't want to share with anyone else. As early as I can remember, I've had a diary or a journal of some sort. When I was younger, I scribbled the names of boys I liked and crossed them out just as quickly. It was a secret place for me to confess.

Journaling is still my secret place for lessons learned and written confession. As a child, I fiercely protected my writing. As an adult, I'm okay with sharing it with others. My journaling shifted when I got to know Jesus. My worldly, egocentric entries changed to Bible verses and God-whispered revelation.

When God talks back, you know the Holy Spirit is present. Don't run from Him. Embrace the wisdom that comes from unbroken fellowship with the Father.

I have never heard God audibly, but give me a good prayer, blank paper, and a working pen, and the Holy Spirit can and will write through me. I remember sharing this gift with my brother. It could've freaked him out, but he didn't act too alarmed.

My brother was in Bible college at the time, pursuing a life in ministry. He came to Atlanta to visit during a rough time for me and my boyfriend of a few years. I had been praying for

God to give me wisdom and discernment in the relationship. I wanted to know if I should move on or not.

Do you ever treat your relationship with God like a crystal ball? You know He knows the outcome, and you want so badly to catch a glimpse of the future. The journal response I shared with my brother that day was like looking into a crystal ball and making sense of something, like a long, drawn-out Dove Chocolate wrapper. Here is what He told me:

My Dearest,

You know Me. You keep learning more and more about Me each day. Keep it up. I have been watching as you want so badly to follow me with 100 percent surrender, but you've always held on to a part of your heart. You've tried to submit, only to grow impatient. And I've made it easy for others to be attracted to you. Your life thus far has been a scattered path of following Me. Your most joyful memories and experiences have come from My call and your action. People are attracted to that obedience and the results and stories that come from a life surrendered to Me.

But until now, you haven't noticed how others (not just your family and friends), enjoy your joy. Those closest to you know that when you're walking with Me, you're fully alive. Here's where the challenge comes into play: those who don't know you are intrigued as well. I've given you a heart for My people, a special heart for those who need Me but haven't found Me. They crave people like you.

You're doing life well, and you know Me. You may think that is typical, My child, but it's not. Even when you think you're not on the vine, you are. Our relationship has grown since you first encountered Me, just as it should. But with that, you attract many who can lead you astray. And you've been led. Not that I don't love the man you're with, but I do have someone special for you. I've been waiting for you to realize I've made you charismatic to all—a wonderful influence and vehicle to minister in My name. But you've been distracted by those in your path who shouldn't have been more than a friend or someone for you to pray for. No more.

I have you exactly where I want you. You're finally healing from relationships I never meant you to have. Now you'll let me bring you back to yourself. You've always been with Me, but at times, you've covered your light. No more.

Now that you're here, know that I put much thought into you, that I have taken you (and allowed you to go) exactly where you needed to go, so you'd be ready for the next step. Everyone will be intrigued by you; I made you that way. I plan to use you marvelously. Your husband is learning his own lessons right now too.

One day soon, you'll both thank Me for where you've been, where you are, and where you'll go together. Until then, enjoy your life—live it up! You have so much going for you!

Don't shrink back. Don't shy away from meeting new people because you fear their perception of you. You are beautiful, just as I made you. I've carried you through the storms of life and, should they come back (they will), I'll carry you again. But for now, go out and be the beauty of My creation.

I've designed you to meet many different souls. You don't want to miss out on those lives and those plans. I love you dearly. I hear your prayers. I'll come through on all My promises—the ones you've read, the ones you've heard about, the ones you've shared out loud, and the ones you haven't. I have a fairytale in mind for you. Don't be scared or ashamed to believe it. I will come through.

Until then, be still, believe Me, and go out and shine your light.

Love you more than ever,
Your Father, God

My brother responded with a mixture of awe and shock. He didn't say much, but I was so passionate about the words God had given me, I didn't care what he thought.

I know the Holy Spirit has wonder-working power. I know Satan tries as hard as he can to interrupt that power in my life, and he does it in yours too. Whether you're new to Christianity or you've been here your whole life, the enemy wants to destroy your connection with the Father. If you're among the lost, he'll try even harder because, according to the Bible, heaven rejoices when a lost sheep has been found (Luke 15:3–7).

My pastor recently spoke on the three baptisms in the Christian life. The first involves acknowledging God, accepting Christ as your Savior, and securing your salvation. (This may sound like three, but it's only one.) You can simply say, "Dear Lord, I believe in You. I believe You sent Your Son to die for me. I want to pursue my life in Christ. Forgive me and make me brand new."

The second baptism is baptism with water—a public proclamation of a spiritual decision.

I love the way my Atlanta church did this. Their baptism testimonies brought me to tears more than once, and I didn't even know the people making life-changing decisions that day. They described their lives before Christ and affirmed their acceptance of Christ before their baptism in the balcony baptistery. Witnessing these stories of lives changed by Christ was a special treat. God had chased them down, reached them, and brought them back to Himself, because He was after their hearts.

Then my pastor brought the third baptism—the baptism of the Holy Spirit—to the conversation. He referenced Acts 1:5, in which Jesus tells the apostles, "John baptized with water, but in just a few days you will be baptized with the Holy Spirit." This baptism has the most power to change your life while you are on the earth. The other two change your eternity, but allowing the Holy Spirit to work freely in your life changes you today.

The order of events for baptism and receiving the Holy Spirit is the same for every believer. First you recognize your sin and repent. Repentance is not a temporary Band-Aid for your sins. It is a true recognition of your wrongdoing, followed by a genuine desire to live a new life in Christ.

When you repent, confess your sins, and ask for forgiveness, 1 John 1:9 tells us "he is faithful and just to forgive us our sins and to cleanse us from all wickedness." You will be forgiven and receive salvation. Jesus died so you can live a clean life.

Next, water baptism is a response to God from a clean conscience. It will not remove dirt from your body, but it will give you a new life because of Jesus's resurrection (1 Peter 3:21). It is the next step in the believer's journey to surrender old ways and choose a new way of living.

Then you will receive the gift of the Holy Spirit. Jesus promised the Holy Spirit would be a guide to come alongside us and give us godly direction. The Holy Spirit can reveal Himself to believers in various ways.

I can speak of the process that works for me, but everyone is different. First, I have to have time, space, and the right mindset before I can hear what God is telling me through the Holy Spirit. Let's work through those, one by one.

First: time. We don't have enough of it. We wish we could be more efficient with it. We run out of it on a regular basis. Did you know that time doesn't matter to God? In the Bible, we learn that "a day is like a thousand years to the Lord, and a thousand years is like a day" (2 Peter 3:8). In our finite minds, time enslaves us. Yet God is not bound by time. I'm learning that time is one thing I do have control over. I can't control other people, my health, or the success of my business (although I can positively impact the last two), but I can control how I spend my time.

I confess to wasting a lot of time. I regularly look for ways to be more strategic and intentional with the time I have in a day, and then to turn that into intentional time spent in a week, a month, a year . . . However, I fail. Constantly. I want to shave down my days until all that is left are the things that matter most: God, my husband, my children, my family and friends, and the lost, deserted, suffering people I pass on a daily basis.

But I don't prioritize those things properly. I spend more time reading junk email, watching entertainment news, and flipping through random home decorating magazines than I care to admit. And you know what? None of those things are bad in moderation. Social media is another time-stealing culprit. Today's culture is so worried about connecting with complete strangers that we lose connection with the people living in our homes. More than that, we lose connection with the God who created us. Most days, I am just as guilty of this as anyone else. I need to change the way I spend my time. I find that is the first key to the power of the Holy Spirit working in my life.

Next: space. You can listen anywhere, you know. Some places and spaces overflow with distraction while others are quiet. When I want to pay attention to what God is telling me (why don't I want that all the time?), I must find a quiet space. Not just quiet, but comfortable. I don't need comfy clothes and a cup of coffee, but they help.

Matthew 6:5–6 shows us how to pray and receive what the Holy Spirit has to offer us:

When you pray, don't be like the hypocrites

who love to pray publicly on street corners and in the synagogues where everyone can see them. I tell you the truth, that is all the reward they will ever get. But when you pray, go away by yourself, shut the door behind you, and pray to your Father in private. Then your Father, who sees everything, will reward you.

I pray everywhere. I don't always go into a room and close the door. I know God hears our prayers, no matter where we are. However, when I need to get alone with God and have deliberate, uninterrupted prayer time, I follow these instructions.

If you are a super Christian, you can probably hear the Holy Spirit through any distraction you encounter. I am not that skilled. When I make time and have a space that allows, I know I will hear from God. Often when I'm driving, I turn everything off and talk to God out loud. Then, if I stay quiet long enough, the Holy Spirit fills my mind with answers to prayers or prompts me to pay attention to an object or song through which He shows me something I need to know. I am not unique. This beautiful gift is available to every believer.

Finally: a right mindset. We must be in tune with what God is trying to say or do through the Holy Spirit. I can have a devoted time and space without pondering the things of God. I can go into a Bible study or quiet time with the best intentions but come out wondering what I just read. Instead of properly setting my mind on Christ, I end up planning what I'd make for dinner. Am I the only one?

We must be careful about this because the Holy Spirit is not a gift meant just for us. We will also bless others if we're in tune with the Holy Spirit and His power in our lives. The Bible is filled with stories of the Holy Spirit directing believers to intercede on the behalf of others through prayer and action. Nearly all of Paul's ministry was led by the Holy Spirit's prompting. With the Holy Spirit, we receive and can develop our spiritual gifts. Then God can use us in our greatest capacity. The Holy Spirit can move us to speak His truth into the lives of others (2 Peter 1:21).

To be open to the Spirit, our hearts must be clean and our spirits right. In Psalm 51:10–12, David asks the Lord for this:

> Create in me a clean heart, O God. Renew a loyal spirit within me. Do not banish me from your presence, and don't take your Holy Spirit from me. Restore to me the joy of your salvation, and make me willing to obey you.

God wants to renew us and restore us every day, but if we never go to Him and allow the Holy Spirit to work through us, we'll miss out on the life He has for us. The life He intends for you is abundant! Abundant living comes from securing salvation, professing your faith, and having a relationship with the Holy Spirit.

Study Questions

1. Where are you on your journey with Christ? Repentance? Salvation? Water baptism? Spirit baptism?
2. Can you pinpoint specific times in your life when you completed each of the above steps?
3. What is your next step toward seamless spirituality?

Encouragement

> Repent of your sins and turn to God, for the Kingdom of Heaven is near. (Matthew 3:2)

> Each of you must repent of your sins and turn to God, and be baptized in the name of Jesus Christ for the forgiveness of your sins. Then you will receive the gift of the Holy Spirit. (Acts 2:38)

> There is forgiveness of sins for all who repent. (Luke 24:47)

Prayer

Our Father and our Redeemer, thank You for the relationship You offer us. Thank You for the opportunity to live Your way.

I pray for those who have never uttered the sinner's prayer. Please lead them to a place where they are ready to ask for forgiveness of their sins. I pray for their confession and belief in You. I pray they would long for eternity with You in heaven far more than anything this world has to offer. May today be a day of lasting change for them. Please bring Christians into their lives to love them and show them how to know You more.

For those of us who already have a relationship with You, I pray You will reveal the next individual steps each of us must take toward becoming more like Christ. Show us, God. We seek You.

In our Savior's name, amen.

Chapter Seven

SEAMLESS ABUNDANCE

I have come that they may have life, and that they may have it more abundantly.

John 10:10 NKJV

CHRIST HAS DONE all the gruesome work for us. He left heaven to come down and become one of us. He lived a short but powerful life, showing us the way to live according to God. He suffered and died alone. But on the third day . . .

He rose so we can live abundantly!

Living abundantly means living with purpose. We can rest in the abundance of the promises of God. That does not mean our lives will be easy or without conflict. It does mean our relationship with Christ will give us a new perspective through which to live a new life. If we read God's Word and use it as a guide, we experience more joy, peace, and blessings than ever before.

In order to live abundantly, we must exchange the old life (lived on our own) for the new life (lived in Christ). We then throw off our sinful nature and our former way of life (Ephesians 4:22). Our old way of life may have been okay, but a life lived for Christ is unmatched.

When we live abundant lives, we devote ourselves to learning all God has for us to learn and practice. We do this through regular Bible study, quiet time, church attendance, and online messages that share God's truth. We can also learn from the people God places in our lives.

I recommend connecting with other believers in the form of a small group. The lessons you will learn about God and yourself in this intimate setting are invaluable. God has a unique way of creating groups where connections already exist; we just have to find them. We find true abundance when we surround ourselves with friends who can help us work through the exchanged lives we seek.

When I stepped into my first small-group meeting, I was scared. I didn't know what to expect. It took me a few weeks to feel comfortable meeting in an unknown place with unknown people. That was ten years ago, and the lessons I learned through that group still impact my life to this day.

Life is busy and filled with worldly trouble. It's sometimes hard to maintain a kingdom perspective, but it's worth the trouble. I struggle with this. I get hung up in the everyday routines of life. Mundane tasks suck my joy and steal my energy. I need to live a more abundant life in the ordinary.

The Bible includes many verses about rejoicing in the Lord always. "May all my thoughts be pleasing to him," Psalm 104:34 says, "for I rejoice in the LORD." Wait. May all my thoughts be pleasing to Him? *All my thoughts?* So instead of thinking about how much I can't stand doing laundry every day, I should rejoice? Yes! When I'm picking up the same toys for the fourteenth time, I'm supposed to rejoice then, too? Yes!

Psalm 64:10 says, "The godly will rejoice in the LORD and find shelter in him. And those who do what is right will praise him." There's something special about rejoicing in the Lord while completing mundane tasks. Listening to praise music while I'm doing chores helps me feel a bit happier about them, because I'm thinking about gratefulness instead of obligation. When I'm loading the dishwasher for the second time in one day, I can choose to focus on a worldly viewpoint and complain about the task the whole time, or I can give thanks for food and clean dishes. Praise music helps me focus on the blessings in life. Isn't that funny? If we want to rejoice in the Lord always, we have to design our lives to support that choice. We will choose to rejoice and find shelter in Him. We get to choose to praise Him.

Of course, we're all human, and we're bent toward selfish desires and self-centered needs. So how do we overcome those desires and needs to honor our Creator in all we do? In order to have an abundant life, we must actively pursue it. It's not simple, but it's possible. We can also push abundance away. I've done both.

Once upon a time, I was a college student. I went to school to become a pediatrician. However, God quickly reminded me of my strong dislike for hospitals and the sight of blood. I wanted to perform well-child checkups, nothing more. Not the type of pediatrician the world needs, right? So after nearly flunking out of my first semester of a ridiculously overloaded pre-med schedule, I switched my major to elementary education.

I was lost. I was doing what my parents, friends, and adviser suggested, but my life was far from abundant. I went to school, worked a part-time job, hung out with the current boyfriend, and that's about it. My life didn't include any of the things Jesus promised would come with an abundant life. During that four-year stint, I cannot recall one person inviting me to go to church or to do anything that would have been a productive use of my time. I could have gone to plenty of parties with other lost people, but I attended only a few. I was empty. My life was empty.

Then I found Matthew 16:24–26:

> Jesus said to his disciples, "If any of you wants to be my follower, you must give up your own way, take up your cross, and follow me. If you try to hang on to your life, you will lose it. But if you give up your life for my sake, you will save it. And what do you benefit if you gain the whole world but lose your own soul? Is anything worth more than your soul?"

I understood for the first time that the life Jesus wanted me to live was the opposite of the one I was living. My new life should hold the fruit of the Spirit: love, joy, peace, patience, kindness, goodness, faithfulness, gentleness, and self-control (Galatians 5:22–23). As I read through all those qualities, I realized I had struggled with each one, on more than one occasion. I still do. But I'm giving up my own way and following Jesus. Every day, I wake up with a desire to be a better example than I was the day before.

Instead of seeking wisdom from my friends or the latest reality show, I seek wisdom from its source—God. I read the

Bible, and it brings reliable, applicable truth. The best I get from the world is trendy, self-serving advice.

Instead of locking people out of my life, now I invite them in. God has called me to show hospitality to those around me. It is a gift He has given me. For the longest time, I was hesitant to have anyone over at all. I worried about not having the right furniture or decor. Today, God has renewed my spirit and has instilled a love of hosting. Instead of focusing on my needs or my fears, I concentrate on others and making their lives easier.

In the past, I felt like God was far away, but He was right there the entire time. The quality of my life was completely dependent upon what I pursued, and I wasn't pursuing godly things. I pushed abundance away by living each day for the day instead of looking for opportunities to be salt and light to a hurting world.

Is today better? I struggle daily with surrendering worldliness and embracing godliness. I want so badly to wake up filled with joy, to live a productive day, and to go to sleep with a smile on my face. When I have difficult conversations with my husband, I want to use kind words in a loving tone. I want to correct my children by getting down on their level, looking them in the eyes, and teaching them all about grace. I want to be a friend who never judges, always comforts, always understands.

I am none of those things all of the time. But when I pursue abundance, I embody more of the fruit of the Spirit. And I find that God is right here all the time, just as He promised.

I pursue abundance by starting my day in praise and seeking God's wisdom. Most mornings, I read a devotional or the Bible, but sometimes I just listen to praise music while I make breakfast for my babies. I continue to pursue abundance by filtering the events of my day through God's perspective. If I feel uneasy about something, I pray or seek Scripture that will help renew my mind. I cultivate a godly marriage and friendships. As a result, I am supported by those relationships when I feel led astray by the world.

The quality of my life depends upon what I pursue. Now I pursue godly things: wisdom, truth, freedom, righteousness, Christ-centered living. But I must do it with the right heart, because pursuing godly things in order to show the world how godly I am is not godliness at all.

I don't know if every Christian goes through this, but I experienced a Pharisee phase in life. Right after I accepted Christ and surrendered my life and my choices to Him, I started measuring. That's what the Pharisees did. They went around measuring everyone they encountered. Sure, I had found the love of God and was ready to live for Christ, but Satan used my pride to keep me in the dark for quite some time.

Today, I understand that each individual is on a journey with God. When He affords us a new day, we get to decide how to live it. He is a Father who cares for our every need but gives us free will to express His work in us.

Prayer, praise, reading God's Word, and my church all help me in my pursuit of an abundant life. Without one of these, my life is out of balance. If I skip prayer, I can't hear from God. If I don't praise, I don't respond to God. If I neglect God's Word, my mind can't be renewed. If I don't attend church, I don't hear the wisdom my pastor shares, nor do I receive it on my own. Your practices of abundance may be different than mine, but I urge you to figure out what they are. When you have, please vow to consistently attempt excellence with the practices you choose.

The abundant life Jesus speaks of is available. He brought it with Him when He came to earth. He died to make it accessible. It's a gift He offers to anyone who believes. In the end, you'll want to look back on an abundant life. Lean in, don't give up, and God will take you to places you've never imagined.

Study Questions

1. Do you live the abundant life Jesus offers?
2. What changes can you make today to move toward more abundant living?
3. Can you identify people or things that keep you from living abundantly?

Encouragement

> The thief's purpose is to steal and kill and destroy. My purpose is to give them a rich and satisfying life. (John 10:10)

> May the LORD richly bless both you and your children. (Psalm 115:14)

> "I know the plans I have for you," says the LORD. "They are plans for good and not for disaster, to give you a future and a hope." (Jeremiah 29:11)

Prayer

Dear God, thank You for the life You offer us, one of abundance and righteousness. I pray we will seek You with all our hearts. Please interact with each of us and show us the way everlasting.

Thank You for sending Jesus to take our place and to die for our sins. I pray we will not take that sacrifice for granted. Because of Your great love, please help us live abundant lives in return.

Please teach us how to be more like You; teach us to live our lives to the fullest.

In Jesus's name, amen.

Chapter Eight

SEAMLESS DISCERNMENT

Then you will show discernment, and your lips will express what you've learned.

Proverbs 5:2

IN THE PEAKS and valleys of our lives, God has the power through the Holy Spirit to give us discernment in all we do. Discernment is understanding things we can't understand naturally. In my Christ-following years, I have always prayed for discernment. I have always wanted to understand. Don't we all?

But full understanding isn't always good for us. Sometimes God keeps things concealed from us, so we will walk in His will. I can't imagine how many lessons I would have missed if God had shown me the end from the beginning.

It all goes back to the garden of Eden. If you've been a Christian very long, you already know the story. Even if you are new to the faith, you've probably heard of Adam and Eve. If not, check out Genesis. The story lives there.

God gave Adam and Eve full rein of the garden, with the exception of two trees. That should have been sufficient. Yet the fall of humanity occurred because of the fruit of a single tree and the craftiness of a serpent. The root cause was a desire for discernment.

Eve wanted to know what God knows. Sometimes we get frustrated because we feel left in the dark. We want to know what God knows too. We pursue God's will, trying to rest in His goodness, yet sometimes we have an unexplainable feeling of disappointment.

One tree in the garden of Eden gave knowledge of good and evil. The fruit we long to taste before its time gives power, security, and control. The serpent tempts us to eat.

Think about all the sin in your life. (If this feels uncomfortable, the Lord might be prompting you to confess your sins to Him.) We can trace back all our sin to the devil himself. He is cunning, conniving, and persistent in doing and encouraging evil.

The serpent is crafty and leads well-meaning people to destruction. But his shrewdness isn't one size fits all. The devil knows our weaknesses and pushes us down where we are prone to fall. He did it to Eve. He does it to us.

Eve's sin wasn't a desire to know everything God had planned for her. Rather, she was tempted to be like God and know all He knows. As we pursue discernment, we must prioritize our relationship with Christ and be content with the knowledge He gives us. God never intended us to see the future or know what He knows. There is protection in the unknown.

When faced with difficult decisions, we must pray for discernment. God wants us to seek Him for wisdom and understanding. Praying for God's peace and provision is biblical. Yet sometimes we feel the need to control things God wants to handle Himself, and then our peace evaporates.

As long as I can remember, I've had a recurring nightmare about my front teeth being loose or falling out. Some people believe that a dream of teeth or hair falling out can indicate a new chapter or a change in your life.

A part of me looks back and realizes I went through many changes during that time. Another part of me thinks the nightmare was a big setup from Satan. Regardless, these nightmares have made me fear that someone in my family will lose their teeth or have them knocked out. When I started having children, I struggled to keep my fears under control. But my imagination sometimes spun off in all directions. God has helped me to trust Him with my children, but it hasn't been easy.

When I became a mom, my faith in God was tested like never before. Many times, I've had to declare out loud my faith, hope, and trust in Jesus, to remind myself that He is in control and all will be fine. In the early days of parenting, I had to force myself to run an errand without my children in tow. I trusted my husband to take care of them. I trusted my God to take even greater care. But the serpent was crafty.

And then it happened. I had a two-hour meeting across the street from my house. Back then, I still believed that if I wasn't home, things would go wrong. Maybe you feel this way too. I thought up ridiculous scenarios, imagining the worst things that could happen while I was away. Someone falls down the stairs. Another one sticks something in an outlet. The other bumps his head on the corner of the table. I don't think I ever told anyone about those secret fears, but they made me sick. With effort, I finally became comfortable leaving the house for a few hours at a time. I knew my husband and kids needed to spend time alone together. So I left for the meeting.

I'd been there less than an hour when I received a text message: *Babe, I think Tennor knocked out his front teeth.*

I immediately left the meeting and headed home to survey the damage. Sure enough, my middle child's teeth were not where they'd been when I left the house, but they were still in his mouth. I put him up on the counter to take a closer look and thought about my recurring nightmare. I was not happy. But who could I be angry with?

I asked my husband a million questions. Whose fault was this? The answer: No one was at fault. Accidents happen. My lesson that day, and the week or so following, was that God is in control, even when things don't go the way we wish or plan.

I took care of my son's teeth and did exactly what the internet's best doctors told me to do: call the dentist, keep the teeth in place, give soft foods. Still, a few days later, when my husband took him to the dentist, the X-ray showed that the root of his tooth was damaged. It had to come out.

He was three years old. I was devastated.

God taught me some important lessons through this trial. First, don't worry. He has it all together, and He'll work things out for us.

Next, vanity is deceptive and worldly. I was worried about my son's experience at the dentist that day, but his appearance worried me more. It seems silly now, but at the time, I cried because my baby would have a gap-toothed smile for a couple of years. According to the X-ray, the adult tooth below the surface was just fine, so this was a temporary setback for him. And he looks cute with that little tooth missing!

Finally, sometimes God protects us by leaving us in the dark. He knows the unknown. When we pray for discernment, the Holy Spirit guides us and shows us what direction to take. If I'd have known my little boy was going to knock out one of his teeth that night, I wouldn't have left the house. (As if his safety depended on me!) But I found that the unknown taught me to take my fears to the Lord. God works out everything for good.

When we pray to understand God's will and discern the path we should take, we admit we don't have all the answers. Faith is hoping for what you cannot see—believing in the unknown. God is good. He takes care. He will guide you in His truth, love, and grace.

Study Questions

1. How do you deal with not knowing what the future holds? Do you fear the future?
2. Is Satan deceiving you in any area? If so, can you turn it over to God?
3. If your worst fears became reality, what would you do?

Encouragement

O LORD, I have come to you for protection; don't let me be disgraced. Save me, for you do what is right. (Psalm 31:1)

Those who trust in the LORD will find new strength. They will soar high on wings like eagles. They will run and not grow weary. They will walk and not faint. (Isaiah 40:31)

Let those who are wise understand these things. Let those with discernment listen carefully. The paths of the LORD are true and right, and righteous people live by walking in them. But in those paths sinners stumble and fall. (Hosea 14:9)

Prayer

Dear Lord, I pray for discernment for each of Your children reading these words. Please illuminate our paths with Your wisdom. We can't know everything, and we don't want to. But when we become impatient, wanting to know the future, please give us peace as we wait on You.

Your timing and will are perfect. You comfort those who call on Your name. Please direct us in Your ways and make us content. Help us to show others who You are. Let love guide our lives.

In Jesus's name, amen.

CHAPTER NINE

SEAMLESS FAITH

"You don't have enough faith," Jesus told them. "I tell you the truth, if you had faith even as small as a mustard seed, you could say to this mountain, 'Move from here to there,' and it would move. Nothing would be impossible."

Matthew 17:20

FAITH IS AN intriguing topic. How can we believe something we can't see? How can we hope for something that has not yet come to pass? How can we live expecting God's blessings to overflow upon us? The answer is faith.

If you are a Christian, you believe in something you cannot see. If you believe Jesus came to earth as God's Son, lived a meaningful life, died for your sins, and resurrected from the dead, you have faith.

If you are not a Christian, you have faith in lots of things too, whether you know it or not. Every time you visit a doctor, you believe. Well, maybe not every time, but then you get a second opinion and believe that one. That takes faith.

You have faith that systems function correctly, even when you don't see them working. Remember the last time you rode in an elevator? I was in one a few days ago. When I stepped inside and pressed the button, I had no fear that the door wouldn't close. I pressed the button for my floor and assumed I would arrive safely. Now, if my elevator had stalled or didn't begin to move right away, I might have allowed Satan to tempt me into believing I was in danger. So silly. So real.

I don't know how an elevator works, but I believe in it. Each time I get inside, I believe it will come through for me. And it does. So does our God. He works behind the scenes, and everything He does is for our good.

"Faith shows the reality of what we hope for; it is the evidence of things we cannot see" (Hebrews 11:1). If you have doubts, the entire eleventh chapter of Hebrews is a must read. It gives us reminders of people in the Bible whom God rewarded for their faith.

If we have faith, we want to be rewarded for it. We want everything to work out the way we hope it will. But when doubts creep into my mind, I turn to the Bible to read about all the times God has faithfully come through for His people. And Hebrews 11 is where I always land.

"It is impossible to please God without faith. Anyone who wants to come to him must believe that God exists and that he rewards those who sincerely seek him" (Hebrews 11:6). I want to please God. And so, I'm sure, do you.

If it is impossible to please God without faith, we must lean into that. We must believe God exists. And my favorite part: we must believe God will reward those who sincerely seek Him.

Sometimes our version of reward isn't the same as God's, but He is always right. One of my former supervisors used the term "opportunity" when she had a new task or challenge to offer someone. "Lyndie, I have a new *opportunity* for you." When those words left her mouth, she gave me a sly little smile. I rolled my eyes. Looking back, none of those opportunities killed me. They all made me stronger in one way or another.

God has new opportunities for us. We must believe He knows what He's doing. If you've been following Christ for a while, but you still think you know what's best, please pray for God to take control right now. The God who made you knows you. He knows everything else too. We don't. Let Him do His job, and don't get in the way. Then watch Him do His work in and through you.

I have countless stories of blind faith. I have left the country to serve a people I'd never met. I left a stable job to pursue the unknown—and with no leads. I've moved across the country more than once, leaving everything up to God. My pastor says, "You can have faith, but you can't be ignorant." We must take care not to cross the line between faith and ignorance. This can feel like a tightrope act at times, but to trust God with the unknown, we must walk with Him.

A tightrope walker has a safety net. Our walk with Christ is our safety net. If the net is not there, the risk is too high. We shouldn't jump out into the unknown without seeking

God's will. If you are inspired by a faith-filled life, start with God's Word. He leads us by faith. Matthew 14:28–31 records a conversation between Jesus and Peter. Jesus shows up, walking on the water, and Peter challenges Him. "If it's really You, Lord," he says, "tell me to come to You, walking on the water." Jesus tells him to come, and Peter steps out of the boat. He takes a few steps, and then he looks down. The wind and the water scare him. Peter's faith is shaken, and he starts sinking. As he cries out for help, Jesus grabs him and says, "You have so little faith. Why did you doubt Me?"

Peter's faith was shakable, and he sank. When our faith gets shaky, we flail about. But if we allow God's Word to renew our minds, if we praise Him and connect with other believers for encouragement, our shakiness gives way to stability.

In what areas do you need unshakable faith? Perhaps a relationship, a job, a decision, or a conversation? Your God is big enough to conquer all.

Recently, God rewarded my faith. My family lives on the main street of a quaint little town. A couple of months ago, our sweet neighbor had a new For Sale sign in her yard. I called Taylor right away. We had no plans to move or buy property, but I sensed God urging me to call about this house. Why? I still had to figure out that part.

I convinced my husband that we might never have another opportunity to buy the house next door. And then my wheels started turning. Taylor and I have dreamed of owning a bed and breakfast one day. Could this house be the answer—an inn right next to our home?

I thought about that idea for a day or so. Then, with my husband's approval, I called the listing agent to find out if the house was still available. And just like that, God took charge.

Our neighbor hadn't yet accepted any offers. One of my sons and I had toured the property during the open house a few days before, but my husband hadn't seen it. I didn't intend to take the conversation any further until Taylor could walk through it. But God had other plans.

Less than an hour after my call, the Realtor called back to ask what I would offer. Taylor and I hadn't gotten that far in our conversation. I blurted out a number.

Then I called my husband and told him I might have just made an offer on the house. He laughed at me. None of this was my plan. I had a dream but no plan.

A few days later, our neighbor accepted my reluctant offer, and the real faith tests began.

In my experience, when God doesn't want something to happen, it doesn't happen. My motto is "Go until God says no." So over the next few weeks, I kept doing the next thing the Realtor asked of me. Soon we had signed on a home we'd never expected to own.

Early in the home-buying process, I sent pictures of the house to my mother-in-law because she wanted to move closer to us. She fell in love with it but wasn't quite ready to move. Now that we have the house, she doesn't have the burden of wondering where to live when she gets here. She can finish out her year and prepare for her big move, knowing she has an amazing new place next door to us.

God provides. When we have faith in the unseen, He shows up in miraculous ways we could never dream of. God's blessings have followed our faith in His will and provision hundreds of times. It is impossible to please Him without faith. He will reward us when we sincerely seek Him.

While this story has a happy ending, not all do. Does that mean God doesn't care in those instances? Of course not. I've been praying for a young woman who recently lost both her parents and is now caring for her younger siblings. A tragic murder-suicide occurred not far from my home, involving a friend of a friend. A few nights ago, my route home was detoured because a one-car accident shut down the road. I learned later that a young mother had lost her life in that accident, and her three children were hospitalized. A dear friend of mine has just been given a terminal prognosis; she's now planning the rest of the time she has left before the Lord calls her home. It all seems too much to bear.

In Matthew 11:28, Jesus tells us, "Come to me, all of you who are weary and carry heavy burdens, and I will give you rest." Yes, Lord, please give us rest.

No one wants to talk about the end of life, but the time will come for each of us to leave this life and enter the next. Those who are in Christ have the assurance that we will spend our eternity with Him in heaven. The Bible promises new heavens and a new earth, a world filled with God's righteousness (2 Peter 3:13).

Since my miscarriage, this verse has often comforted me and helped me carry on with life. The physical and emotional pain of such a loss is real. But I receive peace from the knowledge that my daughter is waiting for us there. What a joy to know I will be with all four of my children in heaven for eternity.

Thinking of death can lead us to dark places. But if we've decided to accept the free gift of eternal life Christ offers, death is just a new beginning. After all, "we are citizens of heaven, where the Lord Jesus Christ lives. And we are eagerly waiting for him to return as our Savior" (Philippians 3:20). Our time on earth is limited, so we should make the most of it. We are a passing shadow, a withering flower (Job 14:2).

If you have yet to accept Christ as your personal Lord and Savior, I submit to you that once you do, your life will never be the same. Life has its ups and downs, but the rewards of knowing Christ are unmatched.

All you need to do is call out, repent of your sins, believe Jesus is the Son of God and that God the Father raised Him from the dead. Then ask Him to be your Savior, and from that moment on, you are saved. To grow in your faith and to find encouragement on your new path, I urge you to read a Bible whose language you understand and attend a life-giving church that teaches the truths of God's Word. When you align your life with God's will, He will show you the next steps in following Christ. May your pursuit of Him be fervent and your life in His will, be blessed.

Study Questions

1. When was the last time you stepped out in faith and trusted God for something big?

2. Are you afraid of death or the afterlife? If so, consider those fears and line them up with what the Bible has to say about them.

3. Do you have a personal relationship with Jesus that has secured your spot in heaven for eternity? If not, what is your next step?

Encouragement

There is no condemnation for those who belong to Christ Jesus. And because you belong to him, the power of the life-giving Spirit has freed you from the power of sin that leads to death. The law of Moses was unable to save us because of the weakness of our sinful nature. So God did what the law could not do. He sent his own Son in a body like the bodies we sinners have. And in that body, God declared an end to sin's control over us by giving his Son as a sacrifice for our sins. He did this so that the just requirement of the law would be fully satisfied for us, who no longer follow our sinful nature but instead follow the Spirit. (Romans 8:1–4)

Prayer

Dearest Lord, I thank You for the opportunity to share Your truth with others. I thank You for the experiences in my life that have led to amusing stories at times and heart-wrenching stories at others. I pray that every word written here brings You honor and glory.

I pray now for those who have journeyed with me through this book. May the lives of those who know You be blessed abundantly and bring You glory. Speak to them where they are and show them how to please You. Equip them to live godly lives and be more like Christ with each passing day.

I pray, too, for the readers who do not yet know You. Thank You for letting them get this far. Please place more believers in their lives and give them courage to ask questions. Increase their curiosity toward Your Word and Your church. Share Your love message with each of them in Your unique way. Lead them into truth by Your Spirit, and help them to seek You so they may be set free.

May the words of my mouth and the meditation of my heart be pleasing to you, O LORD, my rock and my redeemer (Psalm 19:14).

In Jesus's name, amen.

ALSO BY LYNDIE METZ

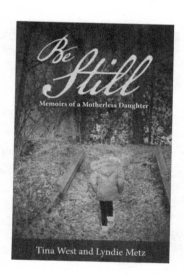

Order Information

To order additional copies of this book, please visit
www.redemption-press.com.
Also available on Amazon.com and BarnesandNoble.com
Or by calling toll free 1-844-2REDEEM.